AF392238

ISBN: 978-978-960-171-4

Cover Design, Typeset and Graphic Illustration by Vitalinks Mega Concepts Limited, Jos, Nigeria.

All Brick Breaker Images are supplied by Pierre and brickbreakerguide.com

Copies are available at special rates for bulk orders. Contact the sales team on 2348189336446 for more information.

Table of Content:

Acknowledgements:

DISCLAIMER:

FOREWORD:

Lesson #1: Think Through Before You Start, Think through While You are At It.

Lesson #2: Make sure that all your efforts are targeted effort.

Lesson #3: Success Could come Faster Than you Expected.

Lesson #4: Sometimes our Efforts Fail.

Lesson #5: Find Ways to Multiply Your effort.

Lesson #6: Celebrate Success and the Effort put in by Others.

Lesson #7: What Happened to our Cause.

Lesson #8: The Rest of the Game.

THE AUTHOR'S VISION.

Acknowledgement:

I like to thank all the people who inspired the circumstance for the creation of this handbook, especially Pierre for creating the Brickbreakerguide.com bringing the game lovers and fans together for fun.

This book is especially dedicated to all the wonderful mentors and inspiring entrepreneurs, hardworking and amazing business owners who are doing a great job transforming the world.

When mud is thrown to dirt you, use it to build your Brick
House.

Forward:

Brick Breaker, Eight Lessons for Entrepreneurs will get any novice started on the path to becoming an excellent entrepreneur with enterprise potential. It takes the basic principles of the brick breaker from the very foundation upward and easy.

This is a manual for every business owner, employee, team player, this tool armed in hand strategically make you fit and indispensible to your endeavour, this book will make you better efficient in recognizing opportunity and enable you with enhanced decision making for efficient performance.

The goal is to find a tool which entrepreneurs and leaders can relate and have fun with to sharpen their skills for personal development and enterprise management.

Lesson 1:

THINK THROUGH BEFORE YOU START, THINK THROUGH WHILE YOU ARE AT IT:

You become what you think about most of the time. The very work you do, whether constructive or destructive is a product of thought. Men from captains of industries to ordinary corner-shop owners over the centuries literarily thought their way into strategic place of authority and power.

Look around you, all that you have achieved no matter the smallness is a product of thought, you imagined even it was a quick-brisk reflection before you got it.

I remember going to an office on a cold call to market a product we were selling at the time and on getting to the office I was a few minutes late, and the manager had gone in for another meeting he was chairing. So I enquired of his secretary if by any chance he usually comes out during meetings and she affirmatively said "he doesn't" I also asked if the meeting would take time and she said yes he is meeting with his BMs.

I understood the creative thought principle, so I told her I would wait a bit and she said ok" so I got me comfortable and sat – I focused my thought on the man meeting me. Well he came out from the meeting and we met and discussed briefly before he went back into the meeting.

Well I guess I should finish the story, he came out to have tea, but he didn't because he didn't know how the tea cup works " the secretary had gotten a new fancy tea cup" the secretary said I was lucky, I said that it is always so with me, I thought him into coming out to meet with me.

Entrepreneurship has been associated with risk or challenges, entrepreneurs must learn to think critically "think outside the box on whatever venture they intend to put in their energy or are already involved with and thinking things into order. In order to put in energy in the right place entrepreneurs should choose an area in which they are passionate about or an area related to their overall goal. This will reduce the stress that comes with wondering if you are in the right vocation and this kind of thought "wondering" is a bad energy - it drains and causes frustration. The entrepreneurs must make an intentional decision to be involved in mind, the birthing of the idea she wishes to use as platform to launch a solution.

In order to overcome obstacle/barriers and ensure success in the end – thinking as a tool must be utilized. Focused thinking help create image of the desired outcome, with this image created in the mind, the entrepreneur would have accomplished more than half the undertaking.

When the image is being figured out, thinking while at it shapes it out to the very end.

Entrepreneurs therefore, must take an informed decision resulting from thinking through. When you stop thinking you start sinking. Think over and over to ensure you understand the details of what you want to undertake to reduce or even eliminate failure in the process. You should also seek counsel from others, genuine mentors who will be willing to aid you in stabilizing and growth. Seek out mentors who have succeeded in the area of your interest. Ask questions to enable you understand the devil in the details. Once you have taken the informed decision of venturing as an entrepreneur. Thinking does not stop there.

The entrepreneur's thinking continues, dedicated thinking on the direction and success of the business – tweaking from time to time to ensure that the business is sustained through thinking through. Entrepreneurs must think pro-actively generating ideas, solutions, modifying the business direction until goal path is established. Entrepreneurs spend majority of their time thinking through on their ideas and ways to introduce such ideas to the public.

Suffice to say there is a thing which steals at the entrepreneur; it is the sin of **PROCASTINATION**, doing later what you can do now or today. All of us at some point have courted this Delilah, the entrepreneur must not romance this evil for so long. It will ruin you as result therefore, I will advice you don't have to think through the whole idea perfectly before you get started, sometimes you just begin with the few tools you have got and while you are at it, you will find the necessary materials to perfect the idea.

Henry Ford

**thinking is the hardest work there is,
which is the probable reason why so few engage in it.**

Thinking while you are at it help to defining the process involved in the venture and enables the entrepreneur make quick decisions because she is in the moment with the undertaking. Critical thinking is to the entrepreneur what water is to fish. Thinking enables the entrepreneur see beyond the now while in the now. As such even when challenges emerges, she is able to endure the testing moments, that moment she is down face flat and battered by hard circumstance. The entrepreneurs must learn to transit beyond the moment into the far future to see, feel and touch the outcome of their ideas. Once the entrepreneur is able to capture this image it becomes establish that the winning is sure.

This might not work for everybody, but the majority of entrepreneurs I met and know have applied it in their personal life. I have also learned to appply this tool, it gives you complete serenity and help you collect your thoughts in one place. It gives you and extraordinary ability for quality and peaceful thinking - MEDITATION.

The entrepreneur should creat quite time for thinking.

LESSONS IN BRICK BREAKER

The game seems simple and anybody could play, until you choose to play then it becomes clear that it is not as simple as it appears. The first step required is to think about it and understand the various keys to press and what capsule contains the points in the game. It could be grasp instantaneously but the player must think through while on the play on the various action and small details which will result in fine win, the player will stay on current moves to know where to drag the track pad to, at what angle to hit the ball(s) and what points to collect or when to Ignore points which do not empower the play. The brick breaker is the ultimate tool for the entrepreneur, it increases the mental alertness and creative thinking strength, it is incredibly challenging yet engaging.

Business should be relaxing at least outwardly since it's what the entrepreneur is passionate about, the entrepreneur invest his energy and time in the thinking to understand the nitty-gritty of the venture and understand when to implement, save or change plans as it concern the venture in order to have a fantastic outcome in the end. Every single item and success in our business, from a beautiful cup on the desk to a month long successful training, is a product of both individual and collective thoughts.

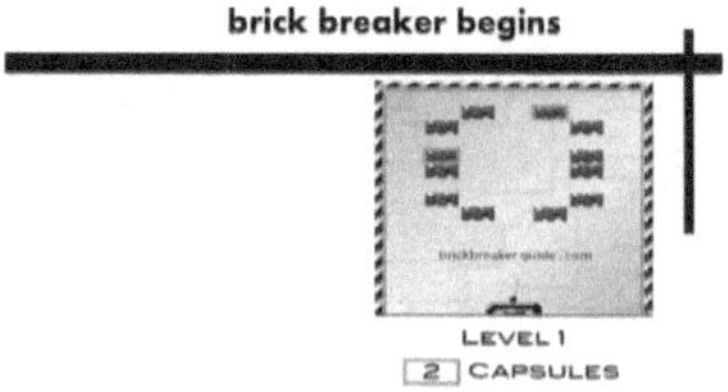

brick breaker begins

LEVEL 1

2 CAPSULES

Lesson 2
MAKE SURE THAT ALL YOUR EFFORTS ARE TARGETED EFFORT:

Thinking is not enough on its own when it is not directed, it becomes worry and this is not healthy for the entrepreneur, it does not empower. The entrepreneur must set goals, make plans, get the right team to enable him achieve her objectives. Once this is done she must put in every effort to ensuring that every team member's effort is channeled to achieving the goals.

Sometimes you have people boring holes in the boat while others are making effort at rowing the boat to shore.

The entrepreneur should make sure that all team members are rowing the boat in the right direction.

To ensure success, the importance of directed effort cannot be overemphasized. What is the use of critical thinking or the formation of teams which result is not to be utilized. Entrepreneur must be relentless in channeling their efforts or their team member's in the right direction.

Entrepreneurs must take caution on what is call self-sabotage, most of the time failures of enterprise are a result of sabotage of the enterprise leader or the key team player's thoughts and actions.

You have heard of near success stories. Have you ever wondered what made it fail? Well in my experience success fails to come through due to a lot of factors amongst which is self-sabotage. The entrepreneurs or enterprise get distracted by the prospect of success and forgets to think while at it. Thinking through while at the job help the entrepreneur to prioritize the important things in the venture, her vision, her goals and aspiration, then putting all the attention required to fulfilled the desire result.

Once the entrepreneur identify her objectives she must be committed to realizing (achieving) it. Any slight distraction even for a second could mean lost for the venture.

Despite this knowledge of concentrated efforts, in a recent time our business got bad, accounts were being closed no new clients coming forth so we got desperate a quarter at a stretch no new client even one. We did some quick market findings, developed proposals hoping to make some quick turnaround – we started rapid marketing off our usual principles. Dissipating energy in the wrong direction, the effect was disastrous in just a month of distraction we lost lots of money. Until we came back to the drawing board to re-strategize and decided to focus back on our original goals and just in weeks we were up and running like a piece of machinery properly oiled.

To help stay focus the Napoleon Hill Think and Grow Rich strategy should be followed: "Write down what you desire to achieve specifying the time bound. Read it loud at dawn and dusk daily, until it become implanted in your subconscious mind THEN FOLLOW THROUGH WITH ACTION. Share this vision with colleagues and be consistent in the massage until team members understand the goal.

Once this is done the principle of autosuggestion takes over and whatever you do will be the result of autosuggestion directing you towards the achievement, arranging all the means needed for the end result.

To achieve the enterprise's goal with team through work, the enterprise leader must indoctrinate the members through communication, clear communication of goals and decisions within the enterprise generally to help the team direct their efforts towards accomplishing the set goals.

The initiator must pay attention to ensuring that member of her team are not distracted by any vision contrary to the organization's goals, bearing in mind that members of the group with personal problems which may interfere with the performance of team should not be ignore – no it should be promptly handled to avoid shake up of the team's inputs.

Amos Agbo

Start with the end in mind and keep in mind the end.

The statement input determines output or every force have equal and opposite reaction – however you decided to see it, it is as it is no Alago. You get out of life whatever you put into, and usually it rolls out in more proportion than you put into it. In putting efforts in to our goals it must be targeted rightly the outcome of which will be ecstatic, otherwise the venture fails and would do so woefully.

LESSONS IN BRICK BREAKER:

In this game the player must concentrate effort in playing right and ultimately winning. Hitting the ball appropriately and when a multi appears – sometimes it might seem like a good opportunity to win quickly. The player must recognize the distraction and focus on the one single ball that will give him the wining game in the end. Otherwise she will dissipate energy to pursue four balls with one trackpad and loose in the end.

Entrepreneurs must recognize this in their endeavors, distraction taking the forms of opportunities and fight it relentlessly through focusing on the main goal or objectives. Team members and colleagues' energies should be channeled appropriately to drive and increase productivity.

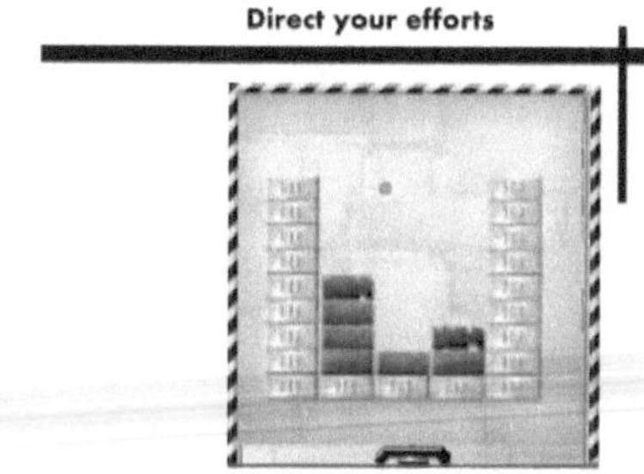

Lesson 3

SUCCESS COULD COME FASTER THAN YOU EXPECTED – YOU DESERVE IT, CHERISH AND TAKE CARE OF IT:

In the game of brick breaker, it is estimate that a standard play of level 1-34 should last 45-55 minutes on the average. Some play could last 35 minutes and that is very fast than the said average. But other play of the same level could last above 60 minutes, having this understanding; every player can come to play with a certain kind of mindset but to win.

Every entrepreneur will desires that she achieves victory over a certain time. Since entrepreneurs are all on different journey, what a player achieved in time must not be the same with what another player would achieve, but could make a player aspire to do better.

Napoleon Hill

Winners Never Quit and Quitters Never Win.

You never know how close you are to winning.

When we set goals and expectation to be achieved in a certain given time, say YZ years period and may be due to happenstance you come about it in Y years less as a result of hard work or a more favourable situation, the experience is good for the entrepreneur, do not waste time wondering how it came about. Instead say to yourself "I deserve it" and take care of the success. When your expectation come faster recognize the victory and make plans for the next goals to be achieved. Whether it comes quickly than expected or not the entrepreneur must be aggressively patient to take opportunity by the jugular as they appear, not to be sabotaged by the thought that it is too early to complete the goal.

Do you say well done and just pat yourself or your team on the back that is it?

Literatures have been written on different ways to achieve success, in virtually any endeavour. in studying this materials you rarely hear what next after the success, it is especially more serious where one invest so much commitment in ones goals and result some in quicker or earlier than expected. Believe me, sometimes either by plain act of miracle or hard work of the entrepreneur success at the goal is achieved faster, here what do the entrepreneur do after this milestone?

The entrepreneur who is committed to achieving result over a period of term whether short, mid or long must at every opportunity put in required or more effort into the goals, this ways success could be attained either fast or as scheduled. If the former is the case then the entrepreneur must accept and celebrate this achievement.

When success comes, the entrepreneur needs to embrace and cherish the moment while at it continue to plan, strategize for the next accomplishment, permit me to say that from my experience the entrepreneur needs to see failure as a flip of success they are both different side of the coins. She must position the enterprise in such manner that even when goals are not met or some kind of obstacles are encountered, the entrepreneur must view this as the stepping stone leading up to true achievement. Seeing things in this perspective will help drive the entrepreneur to accommodate and use the shortfall as a driving force to try again and then succeed.

In this instance success could come faster or later than expected. As earlier stated, sometimes success is achieved faster, then, when success comes later than expected, along the way to that the entrepreneur must have the fortitude to stand along not necessarily alone until the result for which desire is expressed appears.

The point here is that the entrepreneur should be conscious of the set goal and keep focus on the plays that empowers her for the ultimate success.

LESSONS IN BRICK BREAKER:

The brick breaker does not have a time bound play, but players have been able to estimate how long it will last to play a Standard game of Level 1 to 34. Using this adjudged time as a criteria, players can major their self up to this time. If for example a play is estimate to last 45 to 55 minutes and the player concentrated more and had no distraction in the event a great play could be completed within 35 minutes or less. Although, the point to note in the play is the ability to succeed in the play, and while in the process, if success comes faster than expected players usually cherish it.

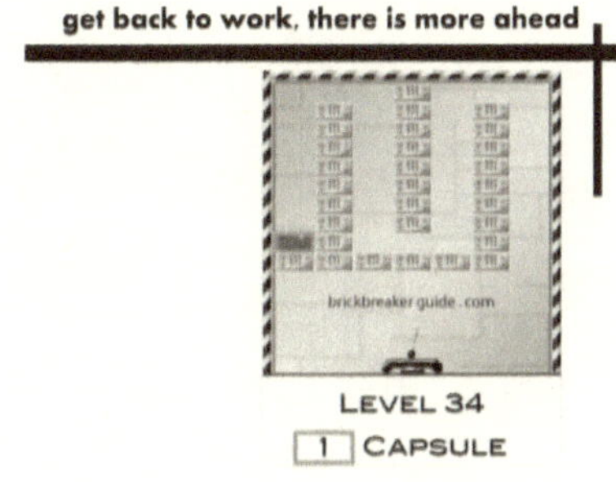

LEVEL 34

1 CAPSULE

Lesson 4

SOMETIMES OUR EFFORTS FAILS, BE TENACIOUS AND HAVE A BOUNCE BACK MENTALITY:

The success story of every great entrepreneur is spiced with the sad tales of failure, brokenness and near quit experiences.

Napoleon Hill

There is no alternative to perseverance, it can not be supplanted by any quality.

Entrepreneurs must belt up to face these challenges in whatever forms they shows up – opposition and misfortune are the ingredient of success it must be handled rightly to produce the expected desires. Along the journey to achieving the set goals, the entrepreneur should build up tenacity and be determine to bounce back from failure or perceived opposition. A Nigeria musician Innocent Idibia aka "2Face" in his lyrics said if I say e easy na set up" meaning if I tell you it's easy, it's a recipe for failure. It will not be easy but until we recognize failure as a stepping stones to either leadership, success or both, without those who are willing to take risks, entrepreneurship will be strangled and we will still be in Stone Age. Failure could be devastating, but to the called it is badge of honour - the price paid. Imagine that Edison hadn't risk failure 10,000 we might have still been in darkness. If Bill Gates had not taken risk with the operating software, there would not have been Personal Computer in almost every home today. The list of men and women who dared to ventured inspite of failure, yet broke-through to success and brought solutions to humanity goes on endlessly.

Hardly do you find perseverance, tenacity and persistence separated from success or greatness. Where one is found in the story, one is seen in the end - they meticulously interwoven to the end.

There is no just alternative to tenacity! Napoleon Hill said, it cannot be supplanted by any other quality. Remember this statement in the beginning of the journey, and it will hearten you when the going may seem tough and slow.

The truest test for the entrepreneur is not the test of faith but the test of success. How best can you be successful until your level of perseverance is weigh. When you fall down, stand up, dust yourself up and continue. Because it is a condition of the mind and never let the physical detect to the mind anything else, nurture your subconscious mind with the anticipation for winning and you will reap the benefit bountifully.

The entrepreneur is going to face a rough trip, literally, mentally, physically demanding, rejection, opposed and tiresome at some point. She must be prepared and learn to recover from failure. Negative event must be viewed as the key elements preparing the entrepreneur and giving the signal that victory is right around the next turn.

Failure seems to play some role of separating and charting the course for the eventual success of the chosen one who will persist. Failure is the bridge which separates the tenacious and persistent fellow who will go the extra mile, the last laps that exhaust men to the point of quitting. Usually the winning lap.

Studying books like Napoleon Hill over six times and from experiences, I have come to realize that the key to growing wealth is persistence. When our efforts fail, some people will take it at face value and quit. It is not failure but the test of staying power and in order to become successful, the application of persistence is immutable. Those, who cannot apply the principle of tenacity easily quits and quitters never win. Therefore, for any enduring success to be obtained, the entrepreneur must identify what goals she is pursuing and set an unflinching, unrelentless focus on the objectives without making compromise to the whims of the old man failure. When our effort fail we should refuse to be beaten or battered by it, through the conscious and deliberate application of the tool "persistence" and refuse to quit by share stubborn attitude of staying with the idea until failure gives up and take a run like an old hag.

After beating the first stage of failure through persistence the entrepreneur must be patient and watchful to sustain the success achieved. The idiot always is right around to show up when you are unsuspecting then your efforts are sabotaged.

The fact is that, there are no alternative to persistence except in synonyms:

Tenacity,

Perseverance,

Determination,

Commitment, etc.

Perseverance is not staying power without working the process, it is working the system to success in spite of opposition or contrary opinions. When we fall, we get up to try again.

LESSONS IN BRICK BREAKER:

The interesting thing about the brick breaker is that, just like real life situation. We all got some life line to always begin real living, and it gives the opportunity to keep living until you exhaust the life line then you can try again. At every stage of the game the player has the privilege of replaying a lost game or chooses to start over again. You don't just quit once you fail, and when you want to finally quit it will ask whether you are sure you want to quit. Life asks us the same question but most of us are not listening.

The entrepreneur can learn a valuable lesson and see his undertaking like this amazing game – failure will show up, you don't have to plan it. Acknowledge it and try again, take another chance or shot at it until you win, until you win.

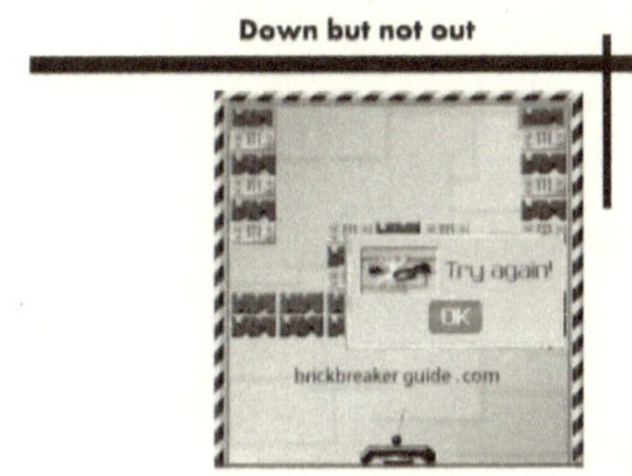

Lesson 5

FIND WAYS TO MULTIPLY YOUR EFFORT:

At the time of writing this handbook, I stumbled on a video circulating on the internet. I think the short video is from Japan or nearly so. There is this kid who was supposed to jump a barrier nearly his height. He kept running at it without success. He got exhausted and was crying "the breaking point" I guess, then the instructor said something in their native language and a handful of the kids who were seated "may be his peer" they were watching. They got up and circled around him, chanted some words - may be reinforcing the lad saying he could do it (jump the barricade) you know, the team kind of boosted his moral and the kid ran and suddenly jumped the barrier smoothly like it was nothing. When I watched this video, I was full with emotion and the thought of what we could accomplish with support from other people.

Vince Lombardi

**Individual commitment to a group effort -
that is what makes a team work, a company work,
a society work, a civilization work.**

Sometimes your effort alone won't get you much, collective engagement is usually profound and all the powerful wealthy entrepreneurs you could think of have leveraged on this principle of effort multiplication. Depending on how an entrepreneur decides to engage this method. In think and grow rich Napoleon Hill called them the master mind group, other times you just stumble on talented people who could add some value to your vision. Be clear about the goal and what you want to achieve with your master mind, get them organized into teams were every member of the group has some exceptional talent or skill to bring to bear.

There are many instances you can expound on this principle, the story of the man who came out to have a cup of tea, well while he was thinking about the proposal we had talked about, his secretary, interestingly had need that matched our product and she belonged to a large network who bought into the idea and the rest was history. She sold to every member of the network which otherwise will be difficult to identify and reached. Here the secretary is like a master mind stumbled upon and become very instrumental, the important point is that she helped to create a multiplied effort which yielded positive outcome.

Whatever ideas, services and products we intend to spread, foot soldiers are required to implementation it. Here the entrepreneur must bring master mind or recruit ordinary people and train them up to capacity to efficiently carry out the assignment of spreading the idea to delivering on the result.

Learn to trust that people will give their best when given the opportunity but I must caution it will not always be the case. Get your family, friends, relations they could be helpful to an entrepreneur with the benefit of spreading his idea fast or increasing sales fast depending on the milestone of her venture. The point is she can leverage on this instrument of multiplied effort by deliberately building networks for her businesses. Family and friends are there to go through the thick and thin with you, then there is the social media platforms and various other networks opportunities, clubs, societies, multipurpose group etc all these structures provide a facility to enable the entrepreneur get an assisted boost in effort.

Leveraging is one of the important skill set the entrepreneur should develop and use to enjoy the full benefit of his or her enterprise. This is because influencing people to give their assistance willingly kind of expand your effort to reach and gain more audiences/clients. As an entrepreneur one is always on the lookout for the opportunity to get people involved with your cause.

In order to enjoy the benefits of multiplied effort, there are key factors that should be put into consideration; this includes honesty, transparency and communication. It is very important to get the people working with you to trust you enough to commit themselves to the success of the endeavour. The result of their commitment (compound effect of effort) is the achievement of set goals and project accomplishment without breaking much sweat.

It is amazing how team have an overall effect on the set goal, how every member of the group choose to drop his her personal agenda for that of the group, working in harmony with every other person in the group for its success.

Together

Everyone

Achieve

More

TEAM work always wins. There are thousands of illustrations to show how team efforts pay off through their motivation of each other and focusing collectively for the ultimate win.

Caution: Be mindful of the people who work on your team – some may really be bad meat, boring holes on the boat instead of paddling to get across. With the proper coordination and leadership any group with the sincere desire to win will win.

When the entrepreneur takes those who will work with them, they should endeavour to sell them the vision and train them up to capacity, in this way she replicates herself to act in different capacity at the same time. The additional advantage is that this principle clears her mind to focus on the more important things and decision making. And where turn over counts, the entrepreneur delivers more service time than he would have usually done alone. And this translates into increased cash flow for the enterprise.

In the game of Brick Breaker, at some point a player get a multi point the balls becomes multiplied and if attention is given to it, win comes quickly because the resulting 4 balls (duplicate effort) each breaks the brick in its path.

Same thing applies to the entrepreneur who is able to harness the power of the group or team, network or social platform to multiply their efforts to enhance the enterprise success.

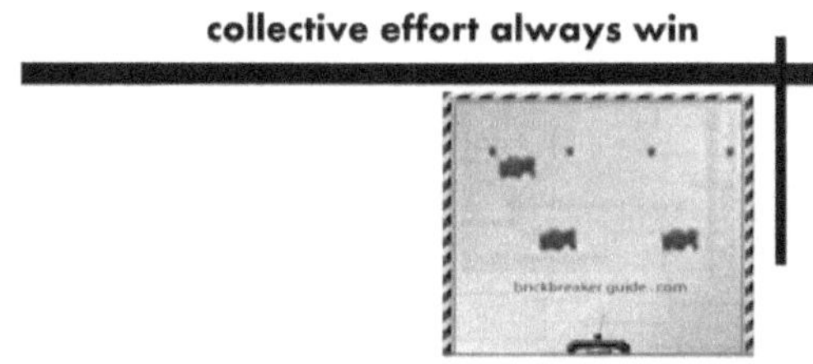

Lesson 6
CELEBRATE SUCCESS AND THE EFFORT PUT IN BY OTHERS:

Genuine success is worth celebrating, more success comes to those who have a grateful attitude towards what have been achieved.

Success is using available resources to overcome challenges and achieving set goals/objectives. It then means that in the entrepreneurial journey every small objective accomplished is worth celebrating. Dance to the small accomplishment, pop Champaign whatever you will do, do it to create fantastic memory.

Efforts put in by colleagues and subordinates should be celebrated.

We celebrate events like naming ceremony, wedding, birthdays we even celebrate the purchase of items like cars, electronic gadget or glamorous cloths, we celebrate certain events spontaneously as second nature.

Celebrating work or business success is usually done in special periods in the office or some special chosen time. Entrepreneurs most often are not spontaneous in celebrating the seemingly tiny accomplishment because they are overwhelmed by the aim to achieve the overall result or some set back, delays and failure in other aspect of the overall goals.

Entrepreneurs focus so much in end results such that celebrating the little success is ignored. In celebrating our success and the commitment others made to accomplishing of set goals, entrepreneurs will gain more because celebration creates bond between celebrants increases commitment to one another to accomplish shared goals. Because the entrepreneur is the enterprise leader, the colleagues and subordinates are invested in the organization to drive it to success. So when the leader shows that whatever success is obtained whether minor or major their commitment is recognized and appreciated, it kind of boosts and increase productivity on their part. Organization and leaders must make it an important part of the enterprise drive to celebrate any form of achievement - above every other thing, it gives the staff a sense of belonging to a happy and fraternal environment.

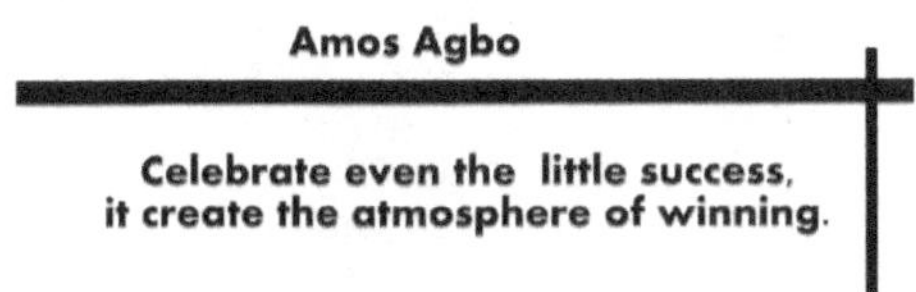

Little accomplishment inspires you to see that there is possibility to get better results; it drives you to achieve more. It is the little successes combined that makes the overall accomplishment. The action of celebrating tiny achievement, also inspire those who are involved with the enterprise to be committed to putting in their best efforts to getting greater result.

I take time to celebrate every little accomplishment even it is as tiny as an update on the computer – I feel grateful for it, and I encourage colleagues and subordinates to exhibit the same orientation because it creates an atmosphere of joy and happiness for accomplishment on the overall goal.

LESSONS IN BBREAKER:

The goal is to accomplish a play from level 1 to 34, and in each level there are various points to gain and lose. Players don't just play a straight game to the end, it is usually required that a player plays each level and win before proceeding to the next stage and each level has its obstacles. When these obstacles are overcome and each level completed it signifies a point to celebrate in real sense.

A player win each level (tiny accomplishment) then finally wins the overall game by reaching 34th level and then the circle begins again.

Entrepreneurs must operate in this fashion, setting minor achievable goals along the path of achieving the major goal.

The accomplishment of the tiny goals should be celebrated until the ultimate win – final goal. Then proceeds quickly to begin another circle of goal, addressing new challenges and each time a new level of a minor problem is solved, it is celebrated to boost morale and commitment to the overall goal.

Lesson 7

WHAT HAPPENED TO OUR CAUSE:

It is very expedient for every entrepreneur to include finances in their planning and goal setting. To include finances, she must ask the right questions like what do you want to achieve? How do you want to achieve it? When do you want to achieve it? Where do you achieve it? To ask all or most of the right question she must think reasonable through the idea she intend to invest herself into. She should map out strategies for success in the chosen enterprise.

Whatever idea the entrepreneur is interested in rolling out boils downs to currency, wait a minute currency is not only the paper, bank notes or cheques, I mean currency including relationships, integrity, honesty, commitment etc. these are the life line that would prove their worth of measure in the appropriate time of need, when the entrepreneur would need it handy.

Amos Agbo

**The world is not lacking in ideas,
it does not have sufficient currencies required for action**

Ideas, ventures and giant businesses in all its forms have been brought to its very heel. Dismissal, frustration, outright rejection can all be traced straight to lack of the required currency of the moment.

The entrepreneur has a good cause, to provide solutions to the current problems and challenges yet to manifest, she is committed to tackling this issues, she talk with passion, every morning she is awoken by the desire to go at this cause, she stays fired up from dawn to dusk, yet without the required currency her ideas will become grounded and extinct. Whatever story we wish to tell about our enterprise, must be around a certain currency, it could be relationships with current or prospective clients, a targeted audience, current or potential market, a certain end user etc. money is not the only currency instrument to an entity, there are intangible instrument which can produce the physical money and those unseen instrument are to be valued more than its physical equivalent.

The entrepreneur should recognize the fact that to carry out any viable venture effectively, currency (supports) issues must be addressed. Therefore, entrepreneurs should save the various forms of currency mentioned earlier in all its forms. Families, friends, also form an important currency tools. There are a lot of opportunities which can be explored, built up and saved as life lines by the entrepreneur.

LESSONS IN BRICK BREAKER:

The brick breaker provides a valuable lesson in saving for the future, the player has continues opportunities to save up life line.

If you look up the unofficial scoreboard of the brick breaker on Pierre site brickbreakerguide.com it is amazing how players rack in score (point) of some hundreds to millions of points, but the most important to note is the lives this players rack in and saved up for fun or daring unfavorable plays and which life lines could come handy.

Entrepreneurs can learn a huge lesson from this, if you have chosen the path to entrepreneurship you must save up currency in its various forms - relationships, families, integrity, honesty and trust as these could be presented as instrument in our venture journey.

Most often times, entrepreneurs are stranded with fantastic ideas, products or services with complete lack of or enough support capacity to push ideas solution through to the next level. Therefore, to avoid the heartaches of having a viable idea yet not having the chance to bring it to sufficient business exposure. Entrepreneur must develop the capacity to save relationship, trust, integrity and network connections in order to exchange it when appropriate.

Lesson 8

THE REST OF THE GAME:

#i.   Apply this rule: In this game it is not every point that empowers the player – a catch, slow; could help the player stop or slow down to evaluate the play and choose strategies that best empower him and create a win.

The entrepreneur also has the privilege to slow down or catch his breath to evaluate and know if the processes are in sync with her set objectives. I call it review time.

During plays the players gains multi and life, these are fantastic point opportunities for the taking, it enable the player to fast track through multiplied efforts or save life line for the future. Sometimes, you'd rather lose the point as it is more beneficial to the overall goal.

Entrepreneurs will find these opportunities in their venture journey, opportunities to duplicate their efforts through leveraging, various aids from families and other relationships. Other times the opportunities could mean distraction; therefore, she must be weary to avoid a fatal failure. Always remember to pause for evaluation.

It is said that "**opportunity come in overall coat and dirty**" I strongly agree. During the entrepreneurial journey the entrepreneur should save valued relationships (important currencies), leverage on people and organizations.

Just like in gaining life and accepting multi or rejecting and missing both life and multi opportunities, there is a FLIP too, it has its benefits and consequences – it could be risky, and it could also be a great finisher for the player. The entrepreneur should be cautious of certain win situation if it is not what it seems but ultimately go with your intuitive gut feeling. "Don't win the battle and lose the war".

The entrepreneur will often times come across opportunities wrapped up in a risky chance – a FLIP, here you take the risk, but remember you can always pause to evaluate the chance and be decisive, you will have another chance of starting over, it's a choice.

Swani Vivekananda

"Take Risks in Your Life"

**If You Win, You Can Lead!
If You Loose, You Can Guide!**

#ii. Be Deliberate About Success.

A player, I mean real players don't just play carelessly, we play to do better than a previous game, and this attitude makes it interesting. What is a play if the previous score is better? Set your mark and be deliberate to succeed with a bigger and better number. Be cautious though, it will not always be about the score for some of us.

Brick breaker players will agree that once you succeed in playing the complete level to the third or fourth game, it becomes relatively easy to keep winning with very few loses. The First Twenty Million Dollars is the Hardest".

Entrepreneurs should be deliberate about success in their endeavour, do not act with a lack of effort you will not get results with that attitude. And once the entrepreneur is able to cross the initial hurdles and inertia, her venture begins to scale higher with few down time.

BE DELIBERATE.

#iii. Know the Place of Family:

This whole affair is just about being "relaxed" and enjoying it in spite of the craze that could with it. Players of brick breaker may be playing for various reasons, ultimately this is just about entertainment to help you unwind and relax, for some it increases the adrenalin rush while to others it helps increase the mental alertness and decisiveness. The game can completely take your attention to a point of reckless abandonment, associates could feel ignored and their presence unvalued. Players should apply self control to know where brick breaker stops and family, relationships and important actions takes precedence.

Entrepreneurs could find it as an important tool for learning and entertainment, acquiring leadership skills while having fun. Family's is important and they have their place by your side not even money can or should take that. In all the pursuit, personal relationship should be accorded to appropriate estate to thrive.

Entrepreneurship pursuit could be crazy, like brick breaker it could be an escape activity if not properly checked.

Entrepreneurs should find a balance between their endeavours and family or other important relationships.

Knowledge is power only when to use is known – Amos.

#iv. Know the Place of God:

We all believe in something higher than us, the supreme, the creator of the universe. I believe He is the ultimate ENTREPRENEUR of all time. The whole universe is His enterprise, delicately crafted into existence.

Man is created in the likeness of God, with intelligence and thoughtfulness. We must learn from the master creator. And because entrepreneurs are machineries for the finishing of creation, working in harmony with God and nature is key to success – We must have a healthy respect for each other, be able to build trust, act in integrity and live peaceable with one another.

In the brick breaker, another game does not interfere with another game neither does any level interrupt another level. Each is programmed to hold its place; this is a result of careful thoughts of the builder.

We are also created to function differently but in complete harmony. Conflicts erupt because men interrupt the flow of nature. Although, like bugs in the brick breaker game, conflicts with human and in business provide opportunity to resolve differences, build better relations, products and services.

Therefore, in order to succeed, we must recognize the place of God in us and function appropriately, whether it is a business enterprise, personal relationships or working with nature.

Amos Agbo

There is sufficient in nature to nurture us all

THE AUTHOR'S VISION:

I am a serial entrepreneur with the burning desire to impact on the African continent through entrepreneurial switch, Since 2011 when the BILTIn Vision was birthed we have been involved in entrepreneurial skill acquisition, providing the most affordable entrepreneurship and skill acquisitions training for women, youths and disadvantaged, empowering them for personal development and national transformation of Nigeria, Africa and beyond.

Our sincere desire is to establish BILTIn Entrepreneurial Institute by 2019, an affordable institution where people from all over Africa and beyond will come and undertake boot camp for skill acquisitions, entrepreneurship, citizenship and leadership experience.

This handbook is one in a series, and we intend to use it as avenues to raise funds to accomplish this task, we therefore wish to appeal to the reader to make a generous contribution in kind, gadgets or cash towards the project. Our funding goal is to raise a minimum of Four Million USDollars to this effect.

To be part of this project BILTIn 2019, make your contribution/donation through a generous purchase of this book for libraries, communities and individuals and or you can provide computers or make recommendation to appropriate agencies for supports. Thank you.